Contents

4
Killer creatures

6
Top killers

8
Wolves of the north

10
Arctic hunters

12
Hunting in packs

14
Swarming piranhas

16
Shark attack!

18
Fierce orcas

20
Venomous snakes

22
Crushing snakes

24
Killer crocodiles

26
Deadly spiders

28
An army of ants

30
Glossary

32
Index

Killer creatures

In order to survive, many animals have become killer creatures, either to defend themselves or to eat other animals. Some hunt on their own, while others work together in **packs** or even huge armies. Killer creatures are found in the air, underwater or on land.

Sharks

This great white shark has grabbed a mouthful of tuna. The great white is the ultimate ocean hunter. It uses its senses, speed and terrifying power to catch other animals.

Big cats

This Bengal tiger is showing off its huge teeth. Tigers, lions and other big cats use **stealth**, speed and sheer power to bring down other creatures, such as deer.

Wolves

Like African wild dogs and hyenas, wolves are **predators** that hunt in packs. Wolves, such as this grey wolf, use teamwork, stamina and speed to hunt animals.

Spiders

This Sydney funnel web spider is getting ready to strike. These spiders bite with their fangs and inject **venom** to **paralyse** or kill other creatures.

Snakes

As this snake bites into a mouse, venom pumps out of its fangs. Not all snakes use venom to kill. Constrictors coil their body around their victims, squeezing them to death.

Top killers

Big cats use long claws, sharp teeth and strong, crushing jaws to catch other animals. They also have sharp senses, stealth, speed and power, making them one of the animal world's top killers. Most big cats are lone hunters, hunting their **prey** slowly and silently. They then sprint forwards to pounce and deliver a deadly bite.

Lionesses take down a buffalo.

Living in a pride

Hunting together allows lions to bring down larger prey, providing food for the whole pride. The males protect the kill from other hungry animals, giving the lion cubs more time to eat.

Teamwork

Lions live in groups called prides. The lionesses do most of the hunting. They approach their prey quietly. Suddenly, one lioness breaks cover to make a kill while the others close in from the side.

accelerate
To move quicker and quicker.

A lioness attacks its prey, a young antelope.

TOP FIVE BITESIZE FACTS

▷ A cheetah can reach a top speed of 95 kilometres per hour in 3—4 seconds.

▷ Lions are the only big cats that live in groups.

▷ Siberian tigers are the biggest cats on the planet. They grow to nearly 3.5 metres long.

▷ There may be up to 40 lions living together in a pride.

▷ A lion's roar can be heard nearly 8 kilometres away.

carnassial teeth in sides of mouth

Killer jaws

Cats use their scissor-like carnassial teeth to slice up their food. Small front teeth called **incisors** pull flesh from the bone.

Deadly sprinters

The cheetah is the fastest animal on land. It can accelerate faster than most cars. A cheetah cannot pull its claws back inside its paws. Instead, the claws work like the spikes on a sprinter's running shoes, helping the cheetah to grip the ground.

A cheetah has a very bendy back, which helps it to run fast.

Wolves of the north

extinction
When a species of plant or animal disappears forever.

Wolves are fierce hunters. Once they smell their prey – perhaps a caribou or an elk – they close in and attack. The wolves bite at the prey's heels to pull it down. They then tear off the flesh to eat.

good eyesight

Wolves fight each other over food.

Ears have sharp hearing.

Lips curl back in attack pose.

prey

Feeding time
The top male and female wolves are called the **alpha pair**. They feed first and then give the signal for the rest of the pack to join in.

8

Bear trouble

These grey wolves in Alaska, USA are trying to stop a hungry bear from snatching their dinner. Wolves and bears compete for food. Bears are big and dangerous, but wolves can kill young bear cubs.

TOP FIVE BITESIZE FACTS

▷ Wolves live for about 6–8 years in the wild, or about 16 years in zoos and wildlife parks.

▷ Wolves live in packs with up to 30 members.

▷ The long pointed teeth near the front of a wolf's mouth are called **canine teeth**.

▷ A wolf has 42 teeth. The sharpest are the fangs and canines at the front of the jaw.

▷ Wolves' diet includes elk, caribou, bison, deer and moose.

How fast?

Wolves are very fast runners. They have a top speed of 56 kilometres per hour. At other times wolves prefer to trot, covering 1 metre with each step. They can keep up this pace for hours, and cover 100 kilometres in a single night.

Wolf runs in the leader's footprints.

Large feet stop wolf sinking in snow.

9

Arctic hunters

Polar bears are the largest land hunters. They usually wait by ice holes to catch seals that are swimming in the water below. When the bear spots a seal, it punches through the ice, grabs the seal and pulls it onto the ice to kill. Polar bears are good at swimming in the sea, where they use their size and power to catch walruses and even whales.

Learning to hunt

After killing a seal, a mother polar bear rips open the body and feeds on the meat and **blubber** with her cub. Later, the bears will roll in the snow to clean the blood from their coats. It is the female polar bear who teaches her cubs how to hunt seals.

Bear paws

Polar bears have huge feet that help to spread their weight over a large area. In water, these enormous paws act as paddles. The paws are also covered with fur to keep them warm against the freezing ice and snow.

fur-lined paws

Arctic
The freezing region that
surrounds the North Pole.

Brown bear

Grizzly bears are found
in the cold parts of
North America. These
huge hunters kill prey
as large as moose.
They also catch fish
and dig out burrowing
creatures, such as
ground squirrels.

large
teeth

sharp
claws

This polar
bear has
grabbed a
white beluga
whale.

Out at sea

Polar bears are excellent swimmers
and can swim out to sea as far as
100 kilometres from land. They can
dive as deep as 4.5 metres to chase
prey and stay underwater for more
than a minute.

TOP FIVE BITESIZE FACTS

▷ Adult polar bears can weigh more
than 12 adult humans.

▷ A polar bear cub weighs the same
as a guinea pig.

▷ Although their fur is white, polar bears
have black skin.

▷ Grizzly bears can run at speeds of
nearly 50 kilometres per hour.

▷ Grizzly bears will **hibernate** through
the winter to save energy.

Hunting in packs

Hyenas hunt in packs and work together to bring down large prey such as antelope and zebra. These fast hunters chase prey over long distances to tire it out before killing it. Other pack hunters include Australian dingoes and African wild dogs.

Dog meat

Once an animal has been caught by a pack of African wild dogs, it is ripped apart. The dogs eat their kill very quickly before hyenas, lions and vultures can steal any food.

This spotted hyena is carrying the remains of an impala in its mouth.

scavenger

An animal that feeds on the bodies of dead animals.

Night prowlers

The hyena looks like a dog but belongs to a different animal family. Hyenas are good scavengers and skilful predators. They hunt at night in small groups, killing much larger prey. They have strong jaws and powerful guts which let them eat all of their prey – even the teeth and bones.

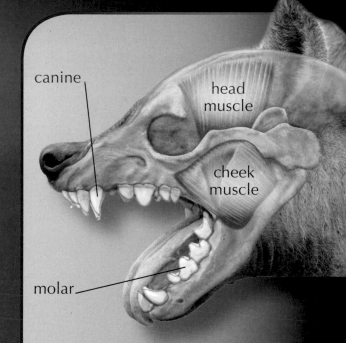

canine

head muscle

cheek muscle

molar

Dingoes kill kangaroos, wallabies and smaller prey, such as this monitor lizard.

Wild dog down under

Australian dingoes are descended from wolf-like dogs. They have been known to attack children, so in dingo territory parents need to be aware of this danger.

Crushing jaws

Hyenas have massive jaws powered by strong muscles. Their sharp canine teeth tear at a victim's skin. Their **molars** are so powerful that they can chew through a zebra's thigh bone to reach the tasty **marrow** inside.

TOP FIVE BITESIZE FACTS

▷ Hyenas live in groups called clans, which can have up to 80 members.

▷ Female hyenas are bigger than males and they can grow to weigh more than 80 kilograms — that's heavier than an adult human male.

▷ Female African wild dogs can give birth to a litter containing up to 20 pups.

▷ Dingoes were introduced to Australia between 3000 and 4000 years ago.

▷ Australian farmers build 'dingo fences' to protect their sheep from the wild dogs.

13

Swarming piranhas

Piranhas are small fish that live in the rivers of South America. They have strong jaws and very sharp teeth. When piranhas are hungry, they gang up in a **shoal** and work together to attack prey, such as birds, **rodents**, frogs and young caimans.

One piranha attacks another.

Feeding frenzy

This young heron has fallen from its nest into the river. Within seconds, a shoal of piranhas detects the bird. Smaller fish take a few test bites, before larger piranhas drag the bird below the surface.

TOP FIVE BITESIZE FACTS

▷ In the excitement of a feeding frenzy, piranhas may attack each other.

▷ Scientists discovered that some piranhas make sounds like a dog's bark.

▷ In the dry season, piranhas can be stranded in small lakes with little food. This makes them more aggressive.

▷ Piranhas' nostrils are so sensitive that they can detect a single drop of blood in 200 litres of water.

▷ Some piranhas don't eat meat at all. They feed on seeds and river weeds.

Jaw is packed with triangular teeth.

Killer jaws

A piranha's teeth fit together so neatly that they can remove a perfect, crescent-shaped chunk of flesh. Amazonian Indians have used the razor-sharp teeth for cutting, shaving and sharpening hunting arrows and darts.

sensitive nostrils

Shark attack!

The shark is the fiercest killer creature of all. This predator has amazing senses and massive jaws. Sharks hunt prey as big as elephant seals. Some circle their prey and **disable** it before the kill. Others make a surprise attack from below.

sea lion

Man-eater?

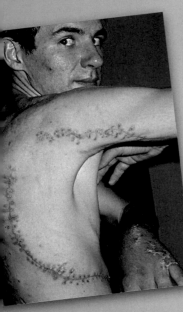

Look at this man's stitches! He survived an attack by a great white shark. Great whites carry out more attacks on humans than any other kind of shark.

Senses

Sharks use many senses to find their prey. They detect vibrations, movement and blood from wounded creatures. They also sense weak electrical signals that come from all living things.

vibration
A rippling movement through air or water.

scalloped hammerhead shark

Gills take in oxygen from the water.

What kind of teeth?
A shark has rows of teeth in its jaws. Some kinds of shark have long, thin teeth like needles. These are handy for stabbing fish and other small prey. Sharks that eat bigger animals have broad, jagged teeth to tear off chunks of flesh.

jagged edge for cutting

large tail fin

Liver helps shark to float.

streamlined body

Strength and speed
This great white shark smashes into a sea lion at a speed of 50 kilometres per hour. Just before it hits its prey, the shark lifts its snout and gets ready to bite.

TOP FIVE BITESIZE FACTS

▷ Shark teeth break or wear out and are replaced by new teeth behind them.

▷ In 2014, sharks attacked humans 72 times.

▷ A great white shark can carry 100 kilograms of flesh in its jaws — more than the weight of an adult human.

▷ A great white can be 6 metres long — that's as big as a large fire engine.

▷ Baby sharks are called pups.

Fierce orcas

dorsal
Something on the top or back of an animal's body.

Orcas, also known as killer whales, are giants of the sea. They are part of the dolphin family and can grow up to nine metres long – that's as long as a bus. These whales work together to kill prey much bigger than themselves, such as humpback whales, as well as smaller creatures, such as fish and turtles.

large dorsal fin

Orca zooms in at up to 60 kilometres per hour.

Sound hunters

Killer whales use a hunting technique called **echolocation**, which is very useful in deep, murky water. They send out high-pitched clicks, and listen for the echoes that bounce back off their prey.

Beach raider

This killer whale has surfed on to a beach, where sea lion pups are playing. It seizes a pup in its huge jaws, then flops back into the water. This is a tricky hunting technique, so if the whale is not careful it could get stranded on the beach.

blowhole

Master hunters

Killer whales use lots of different tricks when hunting prey, including herding and trapping. Orcas herd shoals of herring into a tight ball, then slap them with their powerful tail to stun the fish. Orcas will also head-butt **ice floes** to tip off penguins and seals, or whip up the water with their tail to wash prey into the sea.

An orca hunts sea lion pups off the coast of Patagonia, Argentina.

Sea lion pups are slow when on the shore.

Scary senses

A snake can sense vibrations made by prey through the ground. It also picks up scents with its tongue. The tongue wipes airborne particles onto the roof of the snake's mouth, where special cells send messages to the brain, so the snake knows the prey is near.

airborne
Describes something that is small or light enough to be carried by the air.

Venomous snakes

With its slithering body and lightning speed, the snake is one of the most feared hunters. Many venomous snakes lie in wait for prey. When a victim comes near, the snake rears up and strikes, injecting deadly venom from its fangs.

TOP FIVE BITESIZE FACTS

▷ Snakebites cause about 125,000 human deaths every single year.

▷ There are about 700 different species of venomous snake.

▷ Venomous black mambas are the fastest snakes in the world and can slither at 20 kilometres per hour.

▷ Rattlesnakes get their name from the rattle at the end of their tail, which they use to warn off attackers.

▷ A single drop of venom from a Taipan can kill 1000 mice.

Sea snakes

Found in **tropical** waters, sea snakes are among the most poisonous **reptiles**. Luckily, they rarely come into contact with people. However, the beaked sea snake of Australia is aggressive and carries out 90 per cent of fatal sea snake attacks.

Spraying venom

This spitting cobra is forcing out sprays of venom through special holes in its fangs. In self-defence, the cobra aims the venom at an attacking animal's eyes to try and blind it.

This lizard is about to be caught by a rattlesnake's bite.

Venom

Once the prey has been bitten, venom is squeezed along thin tubes into the hollow fangs. The venom is forced through holes in the snake's fangs into bite wounds.

21

Crushing snakes

Boas, pythons and anacondas coil themselves tightly around their prey's body and crush it to death. These snakes are called constrictors. When the victim breathes out, the coils tighten a little more. The tight squeeze stops the prey breathing so that it suffocates.

Ribs move apart to make room for swallowed prey.

suffocate
When something dies because of a lack of air or oxygen.

A whole mouse

While crushing its prey, a boa constrictor grips firmly with its sharp, hooked teeth. These teeth are not used for chewing. The boa swallows its victim whole.

Teeth point backwards to drag food in.

Jaws stretch wide open.

breathing tube

Stretchy jaws

A snake's jaws can stretch wide enough to swallow its prey whole. A tube at the front of its lower jaw lets the snake breathe.

TOP FIVE BITESIZE FACTS

▷ Boas grow throughout their life. They can reach 4 metres in length.

▷ Boas are excellent swimmers and can climb high into trees.

▷ A large meal, such as a deer, will keep an anaconda full for several weeks.

▷ Anacondas live for 10–12 years in the wild and for up to 30 years in captivity.

▷ The longest-known python was 9 metres long.

Down in one

This boa is gulping down its prey headfirst, so that the legs do not get stuck in its throat. The snake covers its dinner with slippery **saliva** and uses strong muscles to push the food into its stomach.

Killer crocodiles

Crocodiles belong to a group of animals called crocodilians. These reptiles are found in warm parts of the world where the sun heats their **cold-blooded** bodies and turns them into agile hunters. They hunt fish, birds, other crocodiles, mammals and even unlucky humans!

Leathery skin is covered with thick plates called scutes.

Deadly grip

This Nile crocodile has grabbed a gazelle in Kenya. Crocodiles cannot chew. To eat something this big, the crocodile will have to spin around to break the gazelle into smaller pieces.

crocodilian
A member of a group of reptiles that includes crocodiles, alligators and gharials.

Big snapper

The gharial catches fish by sweeping the water with its long, thin snout. Its teeth are shaped like needles and perfect for spearing prey.

Shock attack

A crocodile's eyes, ears and nostrils are on top of its head. This means it can lie low in the water and still see, hear, smell and breathe. The crocodile waits for an animal to approach before attacking. It drags the prey underwater and spins around to kill the animal and tear off lumps of flesh.

TOP FIVE BITESIZE FACTS

▷ Saltwater crocodiles are the largest crocodilians. They can grow as long as 5 metres.

▷ Crocodiles have around 60 teeth. These teeth are shaped to grab prey rather than to cut flesh.

▷ It is thought that crocodiles kill up to 2000 people every year.

▷ Crocodiles swallow stones to help grind up food inside their stomach.

▷ Crocodiles can swim at up to 40 kilometres per hour.

Black widow spider

This female black widow is eating her partner after mating. The black widow's venom is 15 times deadlier than a rattlesnake's. Its bite causes breathing problems and muscle cramps.

Ultra-sensitive hairs pick up sensations from the surrounding area.

Deadly spiders

Spiders are a type of animal called an arachnid. Many spiders use venom to paralyse or kill their prey. The venom is squeezed along a tube until it shoots out through the spider's fangs and into the prey.

Super sight

A jumping spider can spy prey from 30 centimetres away, thanks to four pairs of eyes. The two largest eyes move independently, which is why they appear here as different colours.

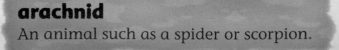

arachnid
An animal such as a spider or scorpion.

This female black widow is much bigger than the male.

▷ Black widow spiders inject their prey with special chemicals. These chemicals turn the prey into liquid, which the spider then sucks up.

▷ Female black widow spiders lay up to 400 eggs in one go.

▷ Funnel web spiders caused 14 deaths between 1927 and 1980. There have been none since 1980 thanks to an **anti-venom**, which stops the spider's venom from working.

▷ Funnel web spiders are named after the funnel-shaped webs they weave.

▷ Funnel web spiders measure 5 centimetres across.

The underside of a female's **abdomen** has a red, hourglass-shaped mark.

Dangerous Australian

The Sydney funnel web spider wanders into houses in towns and cities. It bites with fangs strong enough to pierce a fingernail. Victims must find a doctor fast – the venom can kill in under two hours.

The male is paralysed by a bite and wrapped up in silk.

An army of ants

Army ants march across the jungle floor in huge groups, eating every creature in their path. When an army ant finds its prey, it releases a chemical that 'calls out' to its comrades. In seconds, hundreds of ants arrive to sting the victim, pull apart its body and carry it back to the nest.

TOP FIVE BITESIZE FACTS

▷ Army ants live in colonies containing more than 500,000 ants.

▷ An ant army can move through the jungle at speeds of up to 20 metres per hour.

▷ Army ant columns can be 100 metres long.

▷ In a single day, a colony of army ants can catch and kill about 300,000 creatures.

▷ The ant column follows chemical trails laid down by the leading ants.

Army on the march

This column, or colony, of army ants is moving across the leaf litter. At the front of the column, the soldier ants fan out, covering an area 10 metres wide.

mandible   antenna

head

thorax

abdomen

colony
A large group of animals that live together.

Ant bodies

An ant's body has three parts – a head, **thorax** and abdomen. The head has the mouth, eyes and **antennae**. The mouth has two scissor-like jaws called **mandibles**.

Antbirds perch above the ants, ready to pick off insects fleeing the colony.

Living nests

When the army ants stop to rest, they use their own bodies to build temporary night-time nests called bivouacs. The queen and her eggs are safe in the middle of the nest.

Ant food

Army ants feed mainly on other insects, but will kill lizards and snakes. Driver ants, which also form colonies, can smother and kill animals as large as chickens, pigs and goats.

A large robber fly is ready to snatch any injured insects.

Army ants are blind and use their antennae to sense the world around them.

Glossary

abdomen
In animals such as insects and arachnids, the tail end of the body.

alpha pair
The top or leading male and female animals in a pack.

antenna (plural: antennae)
One of a pair of feelers that stick out from the head of an insect.

anti-venom
A substance that stops the effects of animal venom.

blubber
The thick layer of fat found in many sea creatures and polar animals. The blubber helps to keep the animals warm.

canine teeth
Also known as fangs or dogteeth, the four pointed teeth at the front of a mammal's mouth. Canines are used to grip meat.

cold-blooded
Describes an animal that cannot control its own body temperature, which changes according to the surroundings.

disable
To stop an animal from moving.

echolocation
The method that some animals, such as bats, use to find their way and locate prey. The animal makes sounds and uses the returning echoes to work out their surroundings.

hibernate
When some animals enter a sleep-like state to save energy during winter.

ice floe
A sheet of ice floating in the sea.

incisors
A mammal's sharp-edged front teeth.

mammal
An animal that gives birth to live young, which feed on their mother's milk. Lions and bears are mammals.

mandibles
An insect's mouthparts that are used for biting and crushing food.

marrow
Fatty, protein-rich tissue that fills the hollow centre of bones.

molars
The broad teeth found at the back of a mammal's jaw, used for grinding food.

pack
A group of animals, usually predators.

paralyse
To cause the body of an animal – or part of it – to lose the ability to move or feel.

predator
An animal that hunts and kills other animals.

prey
An animal that is hunted and killed by other animals.

reptile
A cold-blooded animal with scaly skin, for example a snake. Some reptiles lay eggs and others give birth to live young.

rodent
A type of animal with front incisor teeth that grow all the time, such as mice.

saliva
Liquid produced in the mouth to make food easier to swallow.

shoal
A group of fish.

stealth
Being able to move without being detected by other animals.

thorax
In animals such as insects, the middle part of the body, found between the head and the abdomen.

tropical
Regions that lie on either side of the Earth's equator.

venom
The poisonous liquid that some animals inject into other creatures.

Index

A

African wild dogs 5, 12, 13
alligators 24
anacondas 22, 23
antbirds 29
antennae 28, 29, 30
anti-venom 27, 30
ants 28–29
arachnids 26, 27, 30
    see also scorpions, spiders
army ants 28–29

B

bats 30
beaked sea snakes 21
bears 9, 10–11, 30
big cats 4, 6–7
black widow spiders 26, 27
blubber 10, 30
boa constrictors 22

C

caimans 14
canine teeth 9, 13, 30
carnassial teeth 7
cheetahs 7
cobras 21
cold-blooded animals 24, 30
colonies 8, 29
constrictors 5, 22
crocodiles 24–25

D

dingoes 12, 13
dogs 5, 12, 13
driver ants 29

E

echolocation 18, 30
extinction 8
eyes 8, 21, 25, 26, 28

F

fangs 5, 9, 20, 21, 26, 27, 30
fish 11, 14, 15, 16, 17, 18, 19,
    24, 25, 31

G

gharials 24, 25
gills 17
great white sharks 4, 16, 17
grey wolves 5, 9
grizzly bears 11

H

hearing 8
hyenas 5, 12, 13

I

incisors 30, 31
insects 29, 30, 31

J, K, L

jaws 6, 7, 13, 14, 15, 16, 17,
    18, 22, 28
jumping spiders 26
killer whales see orcas
lions 4, 6, 7, 12, 30
lizards 13, 21, 29

M

mammals 6, 7, 8, 9, 10, 11,
    12, 13, 18, 19, 24, 30
    see also bears, big cats, dogs,
    sea mammals, wolves
mandibles 28, 30
marrow 13, 30
molars 13, 30
monitor lizards 13

N, O, P

Nile crocodiles 24
orcas 18–19
pack hunters 12–13
paralysis 5, 29, 34, 45
piranhas 14–15
pods 19
polar bears 10, 11
predators 5, 13, 16, 31
pythons 22, 23

R

rattlesnakes 20, 21, 26
reptiles 20, 21, 24, 25, 31
    see also crocodiles, lizards,
    snakes

S

saliva 23, 31
scavengers 12, 13
scorpions 26
scutes 24
sea mammals 10, 11, 18–19
sea snakes 21
senses 4, 8, 18, 20, 29
sharks 4, 16–17
smell 8, 25
snakes 5, 20, 21, 22, 23, 26,
    29, 31
spiders 5, 26–27
Sydney funnel web spiders 5, 27

T

teamwork 5, 6
tigers 4, 7

V, W

venom 5, 20, 21, 26, 30, 31
venomous
    snakes 20, 21
    spiders 26, 27
wolves 5, 8–9